THEOBALD BOEHM
24 Caprices Études

for Solo Flute

Edited and performed by

Sir James Galway

Southern ®
MUSIC

Contents

Introduction

In writing these short pieces, Boehm gave us 24 miniature gems incorporating the difficulties we face daily while playing the flute. Many of the études require work with the low octave and will demand the revision of the position for the right hand. They are of course difficult to play, but using the method of practice I have outlined, you will learn to play in all the major and minor keys with an unimaginable fluency. Boehm gave precise instructions in some of the studies and very little in others. I have inserted some slurs and dynamics to help you play them.

Breathing

I would like to draw your attention to breathing and what happens when a flautist takes a great breath. Before you take a breath in the middle of a piece, you open your mouth, surrendering your good embouchure. Would it not be better to keep your good embouchure formed, breathing in through the lips and nose? I personally take many more breaths than many of my colleagues.

In most music, a breath is unfortunately marked in only one way, while there are many ways to take a breath. In this edition, the breath marks are of two kinds: (√) being a very quick and short breath whereas (') is a regular breath mark. For a short breath, I would recommend that you don't open your mouth so much, but that you acquire the technique of taking a lot of breath in the embouchure position as described above.

Performance and Practice Notes

Accents (>) should not be forced, but rather be played more expressively and with a good, fuller tone than the notes which follow. Sometimes, I will use the tenuto (-) sign to indicate a note requiring a fuller expression.

Several of the études have to do with fingering, dealing with the acquisition of a smooth touch on the keys. When practicing these studies, you should try at all times to play with a soft touch on the keys, and not to slap the keys as many players do. This smooth touch also helps with a better *legato*. The way to go about practicing these studies is to use a different rhythm. There are examples included with the études below where this method is particularly helpful.

The *Caprices Études* can be broken down as follows:
- Training for the fingers: Nos. 1, 2, 3, 4, 9, 10, 15, 17, 18, 21, 23, 24
- Training for trills: No.5
- Training for tonguing and articulation: Nos. 6, 9, 10, 16, 19, 22
- Training for flexibility: Nos.7, 19, 22
- Training for *legato* and soft fingering: Nos. 8, 20
- Training for lyrical *legato* and flexible embouchure: Nos. 11,12,13,14, 20

No. 1 in C Major, p. 8: This étude is among the most difficult and is aimed at getting a good position for the right hand. The right hand should be inclined to the right with the thumb behind the F key of the flute. This position is aimed at giving increased length to the third and fourth fingers, making it easier to play the low notes of the flute. Try to cultivate a soft touch on the keys, perhaps keeping in mind the difficulties of *Daphnis and Chloe* and the middle of the third movement of the Prokofiev *Sonata for Flute.* Use the following examples to practice this étude:

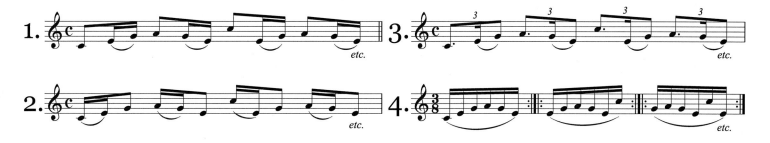

No 2 in A minor, p. 10: While learning the notes of this étude, and indeed any of them, it is advisable to play a little under tempo, using a different articulation and rhythm as suggested for No. 1. In playing studies like No. 2, one often succumbs to the habit of playing metronomically. To avoid this, one must learn to play a little more broadly while maintaining the same beat. When playing soft, try to play *dolce*. These little tips will help you to bring your own interpretation to the study in question.

You will notice Boehm suggests playing the same phrase loudly and softly. His newly-invented flute had much more dynamic possibilities and we need to train the embouchure to take advantage of these qualities.

I have left all Boehm's markings while adding those of my own. You will notice in the first two bars Boehm uses the (>) sign and you have to consider what this means. I feel that it indicates that you should stress the note with your best tone, rather than an accent.

Bar 17 is a good place to begin to play *dolce* and softly. Bar 33 is where you should try to play broadly while maintaining the tempo. Bar 41 is where you should try to play *piano* while maintaining the tempo. At Bar 101, try to play as softly as possible and use the softest touch you can. Use these patterns to develop your touch while playing at a good tempo:

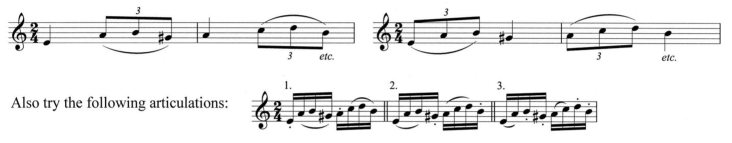

Also try the following articulations:

No. 3 in F major, p. 12: This beautiful study is very good for developing your finger technique. Bar 3, for example, is right over the break and is very helpful for the interpretation of the last movement of the Poulenc sonata. Play it using the right index finger for the B flat.

The whole study can benefit from playing groups with different rhythms. Use the same articulations as in Study number 2. I would recommend using these articulations right at the beginning of studying some of these études. By using these articulations a little under tempo to begin with, you will find you can learn the notes more quickly.

In bars 25-26 you might like to spend more time on this important difficulty, same as in bars 45-46~

Articulation patterns: **Also:**

No. 4 in D minor, p. 14: This is another study in which Boehm demonstrates the superiority of his flute over that of the simple system flute. When you begin to study this étude, you should try at all times to use the correct fingering. Don't be lured into playing it too fast, because of the ease in which the first four bars can be played. Boehm has indicated you should play *forte*. That means with a full tone and not forced. In bars 5 and 6, use the correct fingering and do not be tempted to play these bars with the trill keys. Bar 9 is particularly difficult and you might want to pay attention to your hand position. Bars 13,14 and 15, again, need to be played with the correct fingering.

Articulation patterns:

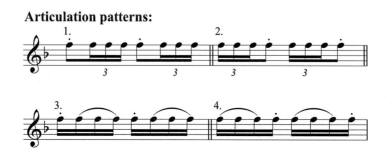

No. 5 in B flat major, p. 16: Generally speaking, people do not practice trills. This is because they understand what a trill is, therefore it is not necessary to practice them. Think what a gift to your technique it would be if you were to practice this little étude. Imagine what it would be like having beautiful trills, fast, medium and slow. Try playing the first 8 measures slowly, having in mind a trill at the end of a slow movement of a Bach sonata or at the end of any slow movement. Then, you have to learn to play quick trills, like those in the modern romantic repertoire such as Chaminade or the fantasias of Taffanel. Don't play the 32nd notes too quickly—they should be expressive. I would recommend taking a tempo of quarter note = 40. Of course, you may modify your tempo to suit your initial tempo when learning this étude. The grace notes should be included in the tempo. You will notice that most of the trills in measures 29 to the top note of the cadenza have no terminations (*Nachslag*). This also occurs from bar 42 to the end.

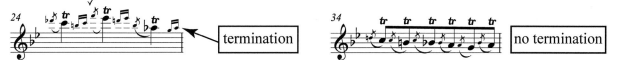

No. 6 in G minor, p. 17: This is a great étude for improving your tonguing. Normally, most études for tonguing are to be found in the second étude of most books, and are in A minor. Not the best key to study articulation. Here in this étude, Boehm shows his genius and understanding of the flute he invented by teaching us to improve our articulation in the key of G minor, the same key as the *Midsummer Night's Dream Scherzo* of Mendelssohn. Try playing this étude with the tongue well forward, as this will help with the clarity of the articulation. You might want to play it with single and double tonguing, varying the tempo to suit your requirements.

There are a few different ways of tonguing, and you might try other studies designed to improve your articulation. The G minor study in the Taffanel and Gaubert method (*Progressive Study No. 6*) can be used to find the best way to play with a broad single tongue. This is a great study if you think of it as a Bach sonata. *Koehler Op. 33, Book 1, No. 9* is a very good study for the different types of articulation. For double tonguing, playing with the syllables Tu-Ku has a better attack, while Du-Gu is broader, generally speaking.

No. 7 in E flat major, p. 18: This study is designed to improve the flexibility of the embouchure. By flexibility of the embouchure, I mean playing each note with the embouchure in the best place to produce ideal tone and intonation. You will notice that Boehm uses dots and slurs. I take this to mean the use of a soft tongue, producing the same effect as a violinist using the up bow to obtain a softer articulation. You may also play it with short notes, single tonguing as well as *piano*. The main point to attend to is purity of sound and intonation. Practice it a little slower, so you can develop your flexibility of the embouchure.

No. 8 in C minor, p. 19: Once again, Boehm returns to the fingering of his flute. The cultivation of a soft touch on the keys of the flute is essential in those compositions requiring the execution of florid passages as demonstrated in this excellent study. The accents I consider to be notes played with a full, well-centered and vibrant tone. In order to make the task of learning the 32nd notes of this study easier, you might want to consider the examples below.

No. 9 in A flat major, p. 20: This étude is difficult for the intonation. You might try playing the scale of A flat to understand the difficulty of a piece which contains the notes C natural and D flat. It requires a very well-adjusted embouchure to venture forth in this beautiful key. When you are learning this wonderful little gem, you might want to try it a little on the slow side and *mezzo forte*. Bars 28 and 29 would benefit greatly from a slower tempo and you could try them *staccato* with a good, clear single tongue.

No. 10 in F minor, p. 22: This étude, along with No. 6, is all about improving the articulation, especially the double tonguing. You might like to incorporate this into your daily practice in the following manner: play each bar separately 10 times. If you find a bar to be easier, then proceed to the next bar which presents difficulty. Pay particular attention to how you hold the flute - for example, the bars with low C. If you play with too much force and slap the low C key, you will upset the embouchure just enough to weaken the note, or even miss it altogether.

No. 11 in D flat major, p. 24: This little *allegro* in the form of a waltz is particularly enjoyable to practice and to play. It would make a pleasant encore in a recital. Again, you could use the same procedure as in No. 10. You might want to practice improving your breathing technique. For the most part, try to improve your short, quick breaths, trying not to open your mouth too much. When you do open your mouth too much, you have to close it again and find the best embouchure for the note following the breath. See the **Breathing** section on page 3 explaining this technique.

No. 12 in B flat minor, p. 26: As well as a smooth finger technique, No. 12 also requires a great breathing technique. Here again, I recommend you concentrate on taking small breaths with the minimum movement of the lips. You will notice in the first bars of this study, Boehm has brought special attention to the main notes of the triplets. Here you have to bring out the melody of the piece. Try playing the first note of each triplet in order to understand the melody and the piece as a whole, while using a different tone color:

etc.

No. 13 in F sharp major, p. 28: This is one of the studies Boehm wrote to show how well his flute could deal digitally with this obscure key. From an intonation point of view, it is really difficult, but mercifully it is slow enough to handle. Before you begin, you might want to play the F sharp major scale and arpeggio to get your embouchure in the right place to continue the study. Don't play this one too quick, but take advantage of the slow tempo. Proceed with your best and smoothest touch on the keys. Try to have your best embouchure for each note.

No. 14 in E flat minor, p. 29: In this étude, Boehm has marked the dynamic as *forte*. This is to demonstrate the difference in volume. Boehm's flute was naturally louder than the flutes which preceded his invention. Play it with a full tone and do not force it. Don't play it too fast, but try to play it in a lively manner, using the first finger of the right hand for B flat through the entire study.

No. 15 in B major, p. 30: In this study, use the trill keys whenever possible. You might even want to practice the trills separately, starting on the trill with no termination while playing them as fast as you can. Try playing A sharp with the first finger of the right hand, and when it is possible, use the left hand thumb. This is an excellent study to learn how to use the left hand thumb and index finger of the right hand to play A sharp, which has the same difficulties as B flat in the flat keys.

No. 16 in A flat minor, p. 31: This is a most beautiful study in a key not often used. Boehm has suggested *piano* for the first 8 bars. Don't try to play too soft, but do try to get your most beautiful tone with a well-focused embouchure. A soft touch on the keys helps a lot to produce a beautiful *legato*. Pay attention to the end of each phrase. When you have a quarter note followed by a quarter note rest, play the quarter note long.

In Bar 9, introduce a more generous tone—*forte,* but not too loud. At bar 21, try to change the color when you play softly. In bars 25 and 26, take time and hold back on the tempo a little to give yourself time to place your embouchure. In bar 27, return to the best *pianissimo* in your repertoire of dynamics to prepare for the good, full tone required to play the major version of the tune. In bar 44, I have suggested an ending to the A flat trill, shown below, and the turn on the low E flat should be slow and operatic.

No. 16, bar 44 - end

No. 17 in E major, p. 32: This is one of the most important exercises for improving finger technique on the flute. Try to learn it by using different articulations and don't play too quickly to begin with. Use your first finger on the right hand to play the A sharps. You cannot have enough training on this note.

No. 18 in C sharp minor, p. 34: Before beginning to play this study, try your low C sharp to get the best tone. This is important as it will influence the the beginning of the study. Boehm suggests *allegro,* but I would advise you at the beginning to learn it slowly, with a few different articulations and rhythms like those we learned in the first study.

No. 19 in A major, p. 36: This is one of my favorite studies, great for developing the agility of the embouchure. It is in the form of a waltz that is commonly found in Bavarian folk dancing. I would strongly recommend you begin to study this étude a bit slower than you intend to play it, especially from Bar 67 to the end. With slow practice, you can benefit greatly in terms of embouchure flexibility and articulation. I recommend practicing all the trills serparately.

No. 20 in F sharp Minor, p. 37: This is another one of Boehm's operatic-style studies. Often, you will hear your teacher say, "Give the notes their full length." Take care in this study to play a long note in bars 2, 4, 6, 8, etc. In these measures where you have a quarter note rest, play right into the rest, as illustrated below. I recommend that you take a good breath in order to play with a beautifully-supported tone throughout. A good breath gives you a good tone, almost guaranteed. In Bar 10, don't play the dotted notes too short, but use a soft single tongue.

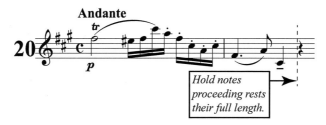

Hold notes proceeding rests their full length.

No. 21 in D major, p. 38: The D major is everyone's favorite, and you can learn a tremendous amount about your fingers, breathing and embouchure flexibility. At the beginning, you should play with the tongue well-forward to ensure a bright and crisp *staccato.* Don't use the same syllables for tonguing throughout the piece, but vary them to give the music a better flow and expression. In Bar 27, try to get a beautiful, soft tone in order to build to Bar 3, which leads you to the recapitulation in bar 35.

No. 22 in B minor, p. 39: In general, play this étude with a good, full tone, though it is a good idea to play different parts of it softly. A lot can be gained from practicing this one especially slow to begin with. I suggest 16th note = 108. This should give you time to focus your embouchure on each note. This étude also requires your best flexibility, and is very useful for single tonguing as an important foundation for double tonguing. Pay particular attention to the intonation of each octave.

No. 23 in G major, p. 40: This is another finger-buster and you will need to pay attention to the position of the right hand to get the best out of it. All the dynamic markings and articulations are from Boehm. You might wish to practice the Taffanel and Gaubert method chromatic scales found in *Daily Exercises No. 5.* They are very easy to master and will help you with this study. From bars 9 through 16, try to play with your best *legato* and soft tone color. In bar 16, you have a big embouchure change, which is repeated in bars 17, 20 and 21.

No. 24 in E minor, p. 42: As in the previous étude, Boehm has supplied us with a lot of information in the way of articulation and dynamics. If you have played through all these études, you will have played in all 24 keys on the flute, and you will have become very familiar with the wonderful instrument Boehm has invented. It is well worthwhile to practice this one with the following articulations.

Articluation patterns:

Sir James Galway

24 Caprices Etudes
for Flute
Op. 26 No. 1
C Major

Flute

B576

Theobald Böhm

edited, arranged and performed by
Sir James Galway

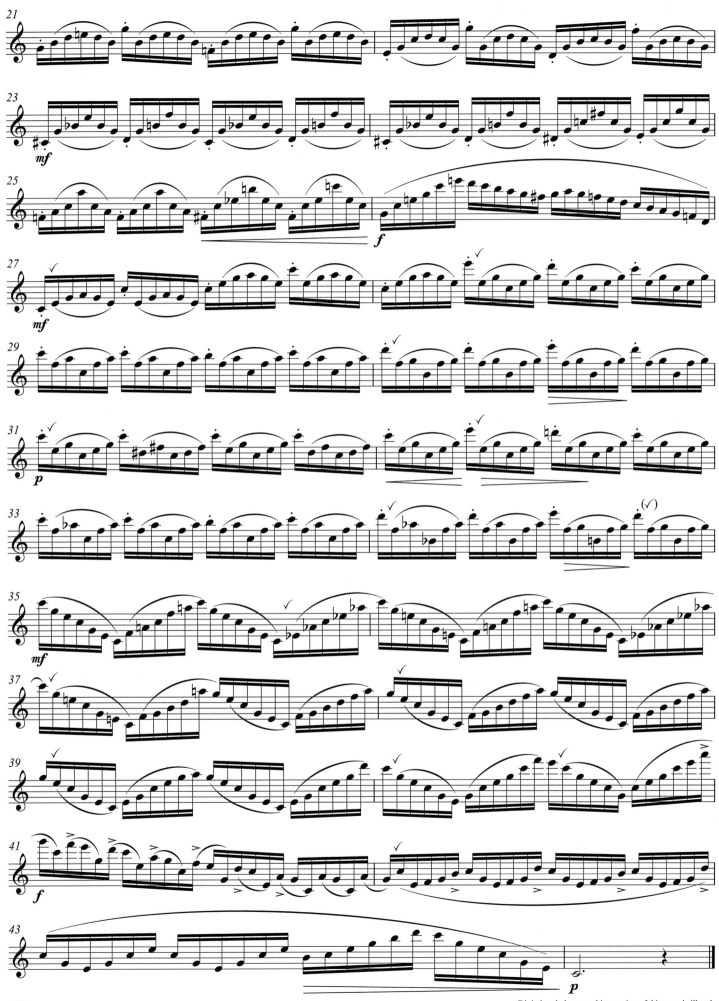

A Minor

F Major

B576

14

D Minor

B♭ Major

G Minor

E♭ Major

C Minor

A♭ Major

F Minor

D♭ Major

Allegretto
Legato, lyrical

11

B♭ Minor

F♯ Major

E♭ Minor

B Major

15

A♭ Minor

Andante cantabile

16

E Major

17

B576

C# Minor

A Major

F♯ Minor

D Major

B Minor *

* this etude may also be played with all notes staccato

G Major

E Minor

SIR JAMES GALWAY

PUBLICATIONS FOR FLUTE

The living legend of the flute, Sir James Galway is regarded as the supreme interpreter of the classical flute repertoire. Through his extensive touring, over 30 million albums sold, Sir James has endeared himself to millions worldwide. Southern Music is pleased to present these new Galway exclusive flute editions.

COLLECTIONS

HL240978 Gilbert & Sullivan Arias for Flute and Piano
Sir James Galway first came upon Gilbert and Sullivan's wonderful operettas while playing with Sadler's Wells Opera orchestra, which later became the English National Opera. His fondness for good tunes, with which the G&S operettas abound, led to this collection, created with longtime collaborator and arranger David Overton.
  This volume contains:
  • A wand'ring minstrel I (Mikado)
  • On a tree by a river (Mikado)
  • Poor wand'ring one (Pirates)
  • Take a pair of sparkling eyes (Gondoliers)
  • The flowers that bloom in the spring (Mikado)
  • The sun whose rays (Mikado)
  • When a merry maid marries (Gondoliers)

HL240979 Gilbert & Sullivan Arias for Flute Choir
  • Brightly dawns our wedding day (Mikado)
  • For he's gone and married Yum-Yum (Mikado)
  • I am a courtier, crave and serious (Gondoliers)
  • Strephon's a Member of Parliament (Iolanthe)

HL240981 Gilbert & Sullivan Arias for Two Flutes & Piano
  • Dance a Cachucha (Gondoliers)
  • If we're weak enough to tarry (Iolanthe)
  • None shall part us (Iolanthe)
  • We're called Gondolieri (Gondoliers)

HL281639 Sérénades du soir
Sérénades du soir (Evening Serenades) is a collection of short, yet beguiling works composed or arranged for flute and piano. Edited by James Galway, the edition includes his own performance suggestions and markings. Enchant audiences with these nocturnal jewels that capture the magic sounds of the night! Works include: Two Chopin Nocturnes and Prelude Op. 28 No. 15, Fauré's Berceuse from ""Dolly,"" and Satie's Gymnopedie No. 1.

SOLO

.HL240977 Briccialdi -The Carnival of Venice Giulio Briccialdi
(1818-1881) was born in Terni, Italy in the Papal States and studied flute with his father until the age of 14. Briccialdi moved to Rome, where he studied composition and was appointed to the Accademia di Santa Cecilia as flute teacher. He would ultimately go on to teach flute to Italian royalty, including the king's brother. He ultimately settled in London and is credited for several mechanical developments which are still in use today, notably the B-flat lever. Outside of Briccialdi's important contributions to flute instrument making, this virtuoso arrangement of this popular theme would become one of his most enduring legacies.

HL281640 Le Thiere -Maritana Fantasy
CHARLES LE THIÉRE'S Maritana Fantasy is a lyrical and dramatic work along the lines of the famous Fantaisies of Paul Taffanel and Francois Borne. It is based on themes from the three act opera "Maritana," the first of six operas composed by William Vincent Wallace. This exclusive edition has been carefully edited by Sir James Galway, and includes helpful performance and breathing advice from the world-renowned flute artist and teacher.

HL240982 Mouquet -La Flute de Pan
With an updated flute solo part edited by Sir James Galway, this new publication introduces Mouquet's whimsical work to a new generation of flutists. In 3 movements: I. ;Pan Et Les Bergers (Pan and the Shepherds), II. Pan Et Les Oiseaux (Pan and the Birds), III. Pan Et Les Nymphes (Pan and the Nymphs)

HL240983 Quantz -Concerto in G Major
One of the gems of Baroque flute repertoire. Features newly engraved flute part, edited by Sir James Galway.

HL240984 Reichert -The Encore Solo for Flute Alone
Sir James Galway became acquainted with this short but brilliant encore of Reichert's while visiting Albert K. Cooper at his home in south London. This new exclusive edition presents the work as performed by James Galway himself.

HL240985 Taffanel -Grand Fantasy on Mignon
Adapted and based on themes from the Ambroise Thomas opera Mignon, this Paul Taffanel work is a firmly established part of the modern flute repertoire. This new Southern publication features Sir James Galway's own phrasing and performance markings in a clean, modern engraving.

HL281641 Titl -Serenade for Flute and Piano
Emil Titl's Serenade was originally composed for flute and horn with orchestra or piano accompaniment. With a lilting Bel Canto style in 12/8, its lyric melody features passages of filigree work that will excite and challenge the musician's technical as well as expressive capabilities. The piece is ideal for contest or recital for the intermediate player. This edition for flute and piano has been carefully arranged and edited by world-renowned flutist and teacher, Sir James Galway.

HL240986 Wetzger -By the Forest Brook (Am Waldesbach), Op. 33
PAUL WETZGER's "Am Waldesbach" (By the Forest Brook), Idyll for flute and orchestra or piano, was a staple of celebrated flutist Marcel Moyse, recorded by him in 1935 on the French Columbia label. ;Since then, it has become a favorite in the flute teaching repertory, perhaps most notably included Toshio Takahashi's famous Suzuki Flute Method. This Southern Music edition faithfully captures this classic piece as performed by living legend of the flute, Sir James Galway.

HL240987 Widor -Suite
Charles-Marie Widor's Suite for Flute and Piano was composed for Paul Taffanel (1844 - 1908), a fellow professor at the conservatory who established the famous French School of flute playing. The four-movement work has become well-established in the standard flute repertoire and is one of Sir James Galway's favorites to play in recital. This edition features a newly edited and engraved flute part with practical and helpful performance notes by James Galv